EVERYTHING
IS WAITING
FOR YOU

BOOKS BY DAVID WHYTE

POETRY

Songs for Coming Home
Where Many Rivers Meet
Fire in the Earth
The House of Belonging
River Flow: New and Selected Poems
Pilgrim
The Sea in You:
Twenty Poems of Requited and Unrequited Love
The Bell and The Blackbird
David Whyte: Essentials
Still Possible

PROSE

The Heart Aroused:
Poetry and the Preservation of the Soul
in Corporate America

Crossing the Unknown Sea:
Work as a Pilgrimage of Identity

The Three Marriages:
Reimagining Work, Self and Relationship

Consolations:
The Solace, Nourishment and Underlying Meaning
of Everyday Words

EVERYTHING
IS WAITING
FOR YOU

Poems by DAVID WHYTE

20 22

MANY RIVERS PRESS

LANGLEY, WASHINGTON

First published in 2003
by Many Rivers Press
P.O. Box 868
Langley, WA 98260
U.S.A.

A catalog record for this book
is available from the Library of Congress

Paperback ISBN 0-9621524-6-3
Hard cover ISBN 0-9621524-5-5
Subscriber edition ISBN 0-9621524-7-1

Printed in the United States of America

1st printing 2003
2nd printing 2003
3rd printing 2016
4th printing 2017
5th printing 2019
6th printing 2020
7th printing 2020
8th printing 2022

For
MARY
THERESA
O'SULLIVAN
1932-2002

CONTENTS

I. CREATION

The Lightest Touch	*Page* 3
Sometimes	4
Everything is Waiting for You	6
The New Nobility	7
My Poetry	9
Before the Light	11

II. THRESHOLDS

Forgive	15
Threshold	16
Fishing	18
The Shell	20
Farewell Letter	23
Once Round The Moon	25
Letting Go	28
Looking	30
Dance Night in Waterford City	32

III. FRIENDS

Firelight and Memory	39
True	45
Looking Out From Clare	48
Richard	51

CONTENTS *(continued)*

IV. MARRIAGE

Living Together   55
Marriage   56
The Poet as Husband   58
The Vows at Glencolmcille   59

V. CHANCES

The Swans at Gleann Treasna   67
The Fox   73
When the Wind Flows   74

VI. RETURNS

Thicket   79
Mariner   82
Sligo Glen: Walking into Silence   86
Sligo Glen: Walking out of Silence   89
September 2001   92
The Bell Ringer   98

[I]
CREATION

THE LIGHTEST TOUCH

Good poetry begins with
the lightest touch,
a breeze arriving from nowhere,
a whispered healing arrival,
a word in your ear,
a settling into things,
then like a hand in the dark
it arrests the whole body,
steeling you for revelation.

In the silence that follows
a great line
you can feel Lazarus
deep inside
even the laziest, most deathly afraid
part of you,
lift up his hands and walk toward the light.

SOMETIMES

Sometimes
if you move carefully
through the forest

breathing
like the ones
in the old stories

who could cross
a shimmering bed of dry leaves
without a sound,

you come
to a place
whose only task

is to trouble you
with tiny
but frightening requests

conceived out of nowhere
but in this place
beginning to lead everywhere.

Requests to stop what
you are doing right now,
and

to stop what you
are becoming
while you do it,

questions
that can make
or unmake
a life,

questions
that have patiently
waited for you,

questions
that have no right
to go away.

EVERYTHING IS WAITING FOR YOU
(After Derek Mahon)

Your great mistake is to act the drama
as if you were alone. As if life
were a progressive and cunning crime
with no witness to the tiny hidden
transgressions. To feel abandoned is to deny
the intimacy of your surroundings. Surely,
even you, at times, have felt the grand array;
the swelling presence, and the chorus, crowding
out your solo voice. You must note
the way the soap dish enables you,
or the window latch grants you freedom.
Alertness is the hidden discipline of familiarity.
The stairs are your mentor of things
to come, the doors have always been there
to frighten you and invite you,
and the tiny speaker in the phone
is your dream-ladder to divinity.

Put down the weight of your aloneness and ease into
the conversation. The kettle is singing
even as it pours you a drink, the cooking pots
have left their arrogant aloofness and
seen the good in you at last. All the birds
and creatures of the world are unutterably
themselves. Everything is waiting for you.

THE NEW NOBILITY

The tawny gold of the first chantrelle
beneath the rough wall of fir bark,
a gleam in the undergrowth
to ignite the eye and ennoble the imagination.
Everyone is waiting for breakfast
to which I bring this husk and holiness
of the newly grown and the newly found.

White plates are laid along the table,
on each of them the omelettes
rest steaming, deep and rich,
the eggs brought from a friend's farm,
the chantrelles nested firmly
in their hot buttered interiors,
and the basil flecked
through them, plucked from the last
tangy stems of a summer garden.

Perfection is a fragile, ice-thin ground
that barely holds our human weight,
one false step and everything cracks
black to the edge. In this perfection
no one dares mention the waters
of the Saratoga Passage shining through glass.
No one mentions our present happiness;
though the last dead century of grief
and misery has barely dropped from our grasp.

Outside the window, the children are playing
in borrowed clothes.   One throws
back her head, sleeves trailing on the ground
and laughs in the sunlight,
and we laugh in witness, for in the midst of history
we are happy like them and all before them.
In their happiness everything still bears our weight.
Timelessness is the new nobility.

MY POETRY

My poetry is all
reversed arrivals,
departures that are not,
secret losses
become public gains
and love welling
from the wound
of a misconstrued defeat.

In my lines surprises
are no surprises
except
the surprise of forgetting
how close we are
to a total disappearance.

That's why I have to say it
and repeat it.
That's why I need to
write it down,
that's why I have
to look in the mirror
and then
sometime after
shout it
from the rooftops
of a blank page.

That's why I have
to surprise myself
and disturb everyone else,
even tell strangers
and people not yet
born or imagined,
that's why
without poetry
it's so easy to lie
day after day
about unbelievable
and unspoken truths,
that's
why it's
so easy to
tell and retell
without knowing
without shame
the same
old broken stories
again
and again
and again.

BEFORE THE LIGHT

I awoke just before light
reached this corner of the world.

Not a glimmer in the quiet cabin,
only the sound of embers settling back
into the first and original light
from which they came, the nugget red glow
of their interior worlds untouched as yet,
still smoored by ashes and the lees
of yesterday's heat.

One touch of that delicate web of coals
with the smith-black poker set against the wall
would disturb the night and all it holds,
break the dark fragile ripening heat
inside everything.

Set me to work too early before the night
has cast its full shadow.

Not to stir then until the tide turns,
not to wake until something parallel wakes,
belonging to me yet beyond me,
not to move until the indefinable
patient fisherman shadowing my life
rises and scents the morning run,
not to cast until the river is imagined
starred with fish and new rain,
not to rise until the body wakes involuntary
sun or no sun, without effort,
without will.

My hand on the latch
the door swinging
open to something real.

The first cold sliver
of moon
ripened from a full dark.

[II]
THRESHOLDS

FORGIVE

I arrived at last, five hours before she died
through airport and grounding fog at Heathrow
and the crowded irrelevance of King's Cross.
On the train north toward her I read the paper
with a close, obsessive, intelligence,
knowing I couldn't face the relevance of the day.
Amid a crowd, we live a strange anonymous maturity
not knowing how deep inside the body,
or how, with each turned leaf of experience
the word *mother* lies waiting to be read again.
In the paper there was no news of her going,
no witness to the courageous continuation
beneath the mask to breathe until I got there.
I travelled as freely in my health as she
struggled mightily to wait, as if we held together,
so far apart, and each in our struggle
opposing corners of creation.
She would let go of her corner
of our world only when she saw me again
for a last time. Imagine then,
the necessity for rest
before the great sweep
of her unspoken life into mine.

THRESHOLD

There were words in the end,
and an unlooked for passionate goodbye,
a song for my father in the few moments
she was allowed to take off the mask,
and my own name said once with the
incredible effort of the last. Then we were all
words, helpless silence, or involuntary
movement in the room, myself telling
her she could go or stay,
my sister saying she was going to meet
the mother she hadn't seen since
she was thirteen, almost shouting
she's waiting for you, the numbers
on the machine steadily dropping
and my father's restless hands unable
to brace the fall. My other sister
ignoring the machine, looked
straight into my mother's eyes,
fierce and unrelenting,
proud of her right and refusal to relinquish
and my mother's eyes equal to hers,
looked back in a fierce companionship
from far inside her going.

Then I heard my own voice again,
as if discovering some marvel
in her face, the knife-edge of a consummate
unlooked for joy, as she turned to go
where we could not follow.
My voice broke from some high
window that was not in the room
and I said look, *look, she's going,*
in unwanted happy astonishment
surprised at the reversal
said as it was, like a young boy
all love and innocent broken promises
anticipating her arrival,
running to a door to greet her again.

FISHING

After her death, I sat by the river
in Burnsall under the sign of the Red Lion
where we used to sit companionable
looking out over drinks and the mellow stone
bridge to the stream beyond,
taking our casual proximity for granted,
shifting easily in our measured
taken-for-granted sovereign rights,
as two people together, still alive,
moving from talk, to silence, to joke.

And I thought of her now
in some bright nowhere
and me left casting into places
I'd never reached before, the line curling
against a sky she could not see,
fishing in the heady flow
for a dart or a glimmer,
just a remembrance
in the moving mirror
and sensing for the first time
the grip of a pure
and flowing absence.

So strange it was
to slip away
in the stream
from a hard won
maturity,
to feel abandoned,
the line spooling,
the bridge gone,
even the ground aswim,
a river going nowhere,
my hook snagging on thin air
and nothing hidden
in the flowing world
to catch, or bite, or tug again.

THE SHELL

An open sandy shell
on the beach
empty but beautiful
like a memory
of a protected previous self.
The most difficult griefs
ones in which
we slowly open
to a larger sea, a grander
sweep that washes
all our elements apart.

So strange the way
we are larger
in grief
than we imagine
we deserve or could claim
and when loss floods
into us
like the long darkness it is
and the old hopes
are drowned again
even stranger then
at the edge of the sea
to feel the hand of the wind
on our shoulder
reminding us
how death grants
a fierce and fallen freedom

away from the prison
of a constant
and continued presence,
how in the end
those who have left us
might no longer need us
with all our tears
and our much needed
measures of loss
and that their own death
is as personal
and private
as that life of theirs
which you never really knew,
and another disturbing thing,
that exultation
is possible
without them.

And they for themselves
in fact
are glad to have let go
of all the stasis
and the enclosure
and the need for them to live
like some prisoner
that you only wanted

to remain incurious
and happy in your love
never looking for the key
never wanting to
turn the lock and walk
away
like the wind
unneedful of you,
ungovernable,
unnamable,
free.

FAREWELL LETTER

She wrote me a letter
after her death
and I remember
a kind of happy light
falling on the envelope
as I sat by the rose tree
on her old bench
at the back door,
so surprised by its arrival
wondering what she would say,
looking up before I could open it
and laughing to myself
in silent expectation.

Dear son, it is time
for me to leave you.
I am afraid that the words
you are used to hearing
are no longer mine to give,
they are gone and mingled
back in the world
where it is no longer
in my power
to be their first
original author
nor their last
loving bearer.
You can hear
motherly
words of affection now
only from your own mouth
and only

when you speak them
to those
who stand
motherless
before you.

As for me I must forsake
adulthood
and be bound gladly
to a new childhood.
You must understand
this apprenticeship
demands of me
an elemental innocence
from everything
I ever held in my hands.

I know your generous soul
is well able to let me go
you will in the end
be happy to know
my God was true
and I find myself
after loving you all so long,
in the wide,
infinite mercy
of being mothered myself.

P.S. All your intuitions were true.

ONCE ROUND THE MOON

Once round the moon
your mother would say
sitting you on the draining
board to wipe your face

as your legs swung like clock-
work under the curtain,
her ritual night-words allowing
you to signal a grave nodded

permission for the cleansing act
and your irritation at being washed
dissolving in the mesmerizing flight
of damp flannel skimming your face

its orbit incidentally cleaning
and shining as it went.
Once round the moon she'd say
and then she'd do it again, hunting

for the parts she'd missed
which of course was twice
round the moon but you didn't
mind so long as she'd said it again,

her face smiling at the very center
of the circle so you could travel
happily round the circumference
of her fancied world,

your own face glowing
in the moon-cold passage
of the cloth and your mother's
voice a safe companion to the journey

so that you were both whisked away
and safe as houses, kept to the task
and let go, allowed to wander
in your mind wherever you wanted

but engaged to comply through affection.
Then, after the cloth had gone,
and like another flight, you'd be lifted up
and over, your nose almost touching

hers and passed around the room to say good night.
The way, the rest of your life you'd be carried
from place to place and person to person,
far from the atmosphere of that crowded room.

The way you return again and again, caught
by tides of affection and remembrance
pulling you back as if you were actually
going forward into a further understanding

of how you were first brought into the world
and then given away to others. *Once round
the moon* she'd say, holding onto you
while setting you on a course far away

into a life you could live as your own
into a world you thought you had created
entirely by yourself, into the realization
she had travelled most of the way before you.

The way there is a trick to everything,
even to stilling a child with love,
the way all necessary work
has an elemental basis to accomplishment,

even the work of remembering
how everything was, that winter night, so long ago
the necessary task of remembering and retrieving
the best that I can think of her.

For my mother, always two jobs, two stories,
two worlds even, in one movement,
love and need and nothing now or ever
to come between the two.

LETTING GO

At the end
things pass away
into a hard won perspective.

The sepia photographs
of childhood
like twilight encounters
with eternity
and the youthful
laughter peeling
across a mountainside.

Standing close together
we make our vows
in front of others
knowing
with a backward
kind of courage
that everything
passes
away no matter
how precious
the memory
and that
even in this
we recognize
the flourish
and the firm
signature of love.

Everything we ever
held in our hands
is given to another
or slips like sand
through the gate
of our fingers
into something
which to begin with
we cannot recognize.
Everything we ever
held in our hands
is given away
in marriage to another
person or another world.

How could we know
the blessings
which illuminated our days?
The joy too strong to feel
until it was
no longer there to disturb us.

We find ourselves
always at last
ennobled by the encounter
the wedding vows
remembered at the end
and cherished now
like a live hand
holding a dead hand
loving everything it must let go.

LOOKING

My mother is a young girl again
standing at the edge of a field
near The Milepost
ready to leave.

Across the field
invisibly, we stand together,
together and each alone,
waiting for her to see us,
her son, her daughters,
her husband.

We raise our hands
to catch her sight
but she cannot see us,
she is too young for us yet,
she only sees the sky
and the green fields beneath,
the way young eyes do
and she looks at the road
leading away
toward us
and feels on her skin
the clear breath of sunlight.

She is made for the world
in her own way
she is life about to make life
she is a youth about to blossom
out of a particular tragedy
into her own kind of triumph.

She is herself
but
she is all of our past
and all of our future too
she is looking and waiting
as we wait,
for everything to come true.

DANCE NIGHT
IN WATERFORD CITY

When you had that dream
in your hospital bed

the first time
we almost lost you,

standing by the door
with your uncle John,

and the whole dance hall
lined with faces

who had known you at sixteen,
it seemed the full tide

of your young life
had swept up to you again

like a long loving circle
of perfect recognition.

How are you then, May,
back to see us all?

And you turned to John
who was laughing

with the rest of them
and asked him what

was behind the door?
And he turned back

and looked at it himself
and said, *May, you don't*

want to go through there
just yet. But in the dream

you knew you wanted
to open the door

and when you found
yourself leaning down

on the handle
as if to go through

you felt
those two hands

firmly in the middle
of your back

and didn't John
push you from the door

with such a full
determination

that it woke you up,
and there we all were

[33]

round your bed
to welcome you back

and that was
the moment

you started to get better
so that thanks to John

we had three more years
and thanks to the lot of them

all gathered to meet you
we know you might have been met now

and are well taken care of
and that somewhere

at the bottom of the dark well
of our going there's another

door of hospitality,
another recognition

that the old intuitions
may be true

about being watched over
and that the timing

of it all is not entirely
in our hands but held

in common with every
other hand we touch

and that the first revelation
after death might be

some kind of gathering,
the first summation something like

a dance night in Waterford City
at the height of our youth,

the tide of faces
ready to meet and welcome us back,

our old body and our young
body, in one body,

greeting and meeting, half aware
and half unaware

of going or returning, the hands pressing
you back to our world

or the door opening this time
to a new light,

an astonishment of welcomes
a surprise party,

the true dream beneath the first dream.

[III]

FRIENDS

FIRELIGHT AND MEMORY
(For Michael)

The way the fire held in the grate
from day to day through that long winter,
you'd think the black coal was nestled
in the flames by invisible hands,
because in my memory we barely stirred
from talking. That year I came back
from the islands the hearth blazed
through a whole winter of listening
and telling. You leaning forward
toward the warmth, hand raised
just like mine is now above the page
so your palm cupped and held
the glowing fire, and your forehead creased
with bearing down on the issue
until you had it just right in your mind
and could feel it beginning to grow in mine.

Outside, the long valley of the Ogwen
was full of wind and bending trees,
night after November night in those cold rains
our minds grew numb to the outside sky
and we drew together for warmth
like the sheep huddled
in twos or threes about the farm
hugging the walls and the frost scoured hollows.
Our faces were lit by the fire but our backs
like theirs were turned to the outside gale.
Inside, the talk fought hard against that dark,
the gales a constant backdrop
to our exploratory wintering blather.

That winter we spent together
in front of the endless fire
everything we said seemed
necessary and important.
I see you still talking now,
looking back to me
over your shoulder
from the kitchen counter,
the teapot in your left hand
while the kettle bubbled
and steamed in your right,
carrying the point of the argument
through every movement,
until the final satisfying
set of the lid in the pot.

You wanted to know, you said,
if Blake was true in his meeting
with the angels or had exaggerated
an intuition to make the point we stand
in conversation with worlds
larger than ourselves. I loved the
youthful argument then,
but sense now, looking back
haunting possibilities
to that final enquiry
so that affirmation or negation
of your repeated question
has enormous consequence
and you stand there
right across my past
as if blocking further access
to my future,

looking in me for a truth
I am not yet ready to know.
In that kitchen, you
still keep on talking,
and I, remembering you
year after year,
keep listening.

But then it was almost always
my enthusiastic talk
to your concentrated listening,
night after night, until
our November acquaintance eased
by January into firm friendship,
and I remember one midnight
the exact moment we
first recognized a companionship
that remained solid for a lifetime,
laughing and raising
the winking glasses and in a delight at odds
with the shrieking through the trees,
we fell into a mutual discovery of lines
each of us had memorized alone,
our faces glowing equally with brandy,
bravo lines of Blake and the leaping fire.

We walked the hills in short bursts
between stinging showers, boiled
the few eggs the hens could muster
to an exact softness we thought
could bring a best beginning
and a rightness to the day.

We, with barely a hint of spring in that
sharp air, in the very cellar of winter
and snugged off from the tumult of the world,
were living out a summer of our friendship.
And I know now, like every other summer
in my northern memory, too short,
too much belonging to close affections,
too untouchable by the present,
and not recalled or remembered enough.

After that, just a few memories
more of you ghost through my mind,
like the sun's last rays passing over
the spread, red, bracken
of a Welsh September,
then right above the ridge
at Tan-y-Garth
I see your quick distant walking
silhouette, and you are gone.

I woke this morning
with those lit memories living
in my mind, and now
recalling you, the warmth
from that fire still heats my face
and has me look across
the empty grate to find you.
Your eyes half closed in concentration,
and your face raised, I see you
forever framed in firelight and now

I cannot tell if your serious angel
visits me through distant memory
or close proximity. You are there then,
in that time so utterly, that my present
seems stillborn, waiting, catching
its breath, for you to finish your sentence.
So strange that you should arrest me so,
your point always being that every corner
of creation sings its own aliveness
and speaks to us in tongues
we are afraid to learn.

Memory convinces me
you are as alive now as you were then,
me on this side, you on the other,
the fire now burning between us
the one that separates my life
from your death. This fire
lights my face on one side
and yours on the other
and I see my fear
at making a future transition
to your rested habitation
is a deep puzzle that frets you.
You want to know my fear
and you see in my face
a need for your persuasion.

I find the depth of our friendship
with you gone
has terrible consequences

and makes me think
of the possibilities of a life to come.
You make me long for a future
in which our past together
is still alive.

I put the pen to rest
on the table and turn
to hear
your imagined invitation.
By an empty grate
I try to trust again to your
companionship.

My idea of faith this morning
you and I by some bright fire,
knowing as I look at you, that
even in my own disappearance,
which now must follow yours,
our friendship will leave an essence
and a burning trace, proof against
the winter of any disappearance,
some fiery invisible signature
written together, passed down,
passed on, and by its invitation
to others, a testament and a mark
of friendship; a surety, that holding
the hand of another is always, always,
always, how we get through.

TRUE

Joel, God bless you,
you were wild
as a March Hare
but brought
a spring scent
of fine revelation
to that troubled winter
I first met you.

I am thinking of the way
your talks were always
larger than their titles,
they were apprenticeships
to fate, dialogues with a destiny
always two steps ahead
of easy explanation.
On stage or at the table,
building a passionate theme
you made it personal,
something we had left or neglected,
something we could
if we had the nerve,
touch again, you moved us
through insight or insult,
you trusted friendship
exactly because you were
careless of it and knew
the same robustness that
could break a bond,
could strengthen it,
deepen it, reinvent it
and bind those who felt it.

Joel, I think I love more
than anything
a real conversation—
I will miss you,
you were untamable by the world
in which you worked,
you stood at some frontier
we wanted for ourselves.
In my mind you stand there now
refusing to give up,
humorous but unbending,
engaging God to understand
the nature of his betrayal.

We allow it of you because
you always did trust
that dangerous edge in conversation,
the wild assertion, the sheer
hell with it nature of existence.
You didn't care, exactly because
you cared too much.

Your passion was our privilege.
You were a Whitman
of your world and
I salute you and thank you
in the style necessary
to your faith. I imagine
you here in your old way
looking over my shoulder
to make a summary,
a last line, by way of parting.
Something, wild,
ungovernable
and true.

LOOKING OUT FROM CLARE
For John O'Donohue

There's a great spring in you
all bud and blossom
and March laughter
I've always loved.

Your face framed
against the bay
and the whisper
of some arriving joke
playing at the mouth,
your lightning raid
on the eternal
melting the serious line
to absurdity.

I look round and see
the last days of winter
broken away
for all those
listening or watching,
all come to life now
with the first
pale sun on their face
for many a month,
remembering how to laugh.

But most of all I love
the heft and weight
and swing of that sea
behind it all, some other tide
racing toward the shore,
or receding to the calmness
where no light or laughter
lives for long.

The way you surface
from those atmospheres
again and again,
your emergence seems to make
you a lover of horizons
but your visitation
of darkness shows.

Then away from you
I can see you only alone
on the strand
walking to the sea
on the north shore of Clare
toward the end
of an unendurable winter
as if taking your first swim
of the year.

The March scald
of cold ocean
even in May about to tighten
and bud you into spring.
You look across
the mountains in Connemara
framing, only for now,
your horizon.
You look and look, and look
beyond all looking.

RICHARD
(For Philippa)

When I open the door
you'll be standing there as solid
and as real as you always were,

the silhouette of the hills
you loved to walk
just behind your shoulder

and the corners of your mouth
playing the unspoken invitation
until you break into a smile.

And of course I'll come with you
walking and talking as we always did
while the dusk and the dew

gather in the trees
until we reach the place
appointed by silence

where you have to go on
without me, to another
friendship, another invisible

marriage to which we both
apprenticed and to which
you recall me

when you turn
and look back
with the faith

I'll need to find you again.
Your face and hands
and words all farewell

and future invitation
behind you in the sky the star
I must follow

and the broad heaven
of my further
unfolding. Under this sky

you leave me shy again
and wondering,
remembering with what love

you came to me
at our first meeting
and our last parting.

Twice now you
have made me a bride
to my future life.

[IV]
MARRIAGE

LIVING TOGETHER

We are like children in the master's violin shop
not yet allowed to touch the tiny planes or the rare wood
but given brooms to sweep the farthest corners
of the room, to gather shavings, mop spilled resins
and watch with apprehension the tender curves
emerging from apprenticed hands. The master
rarely shows himself but whenever he does demonstrates
a concentrated ease so different from the wilful accumulation
of experience we have come to expect,
a stripping away, a direct appreciation of all the elements
we are bound, one day, to find beneath our hands.
He stands in our minds so clearly now, his confident back
caught in the light from pale clerestory windows
and we note the way the slight tremor of his palms
disappears the moment they encounter wood.

In this light we hunger for maturity, see it not as stasis
but a form of love. We want the stillness and confidence
of age, the space between self and all the objects of the world
honoured and defined, the possibility that everything
left alone can ripen of its own accord,
all passionate transformations arranged only
through innocent meetings, one to another,
the way we see resin allowed to seep into the wood
in the wood's own secret time. We intuit our natures
becoming resonant with one another according
to the grain of the way we are made. Nothing forced
or wanted until it ripens in our own expectant hands.
But for now, in the busy room, we stand in the child's
first shy witness of one another, and see ourselves again,
gladly and always, falling in love with our future.

MARRIAGE

(Ulysses)

This skin I should shed,
beneath it I am barely visible
cannot be seen or recognized
or welcomed back,
all you can see are my travels
and they are the least of me,
not the one who has arrived.

I am almost home now.
And you, you are always waiting
beyond that horizon
I must make for myself
again and again.

You have always waited
and with your clear eyes,
have always known the secret,
how we wait, day by day
for the arrival of an
affection we must first
have made completely our own.

(Penelope)

It has taken ten years
Ulysses,
skimming the waves,
barely touching
that heroic existence
assigned to you without
your informed
and happy consent.

You are almost home,
get down
on your knees and kiss
the grit and sand of Ithaca.

THE POET AS HUSBAND

I write in a small shadowed corner
in order to bear light into the world,
though the light is not my own.
My darkness is no darkness to you
and nothing you should wish upon yourself,
but my light shall also be your light,
in which we shall see differently
but gloriously. I am not lame inside me,
no matter that I drag my foot, I have run here
through all my infirmities to bring you news
of a battle already won. Let my last breath
speak victory into the world. The race is run
and shall be run again, joyfully, and you shall
run with me, the territory opened
to us like returned laughter
or remembered childhood. Remember,
I was here, and you were here,
and together we made a world.

THE VOWS AT
GLENCOLMCILLE

It's as if the solid
green of the valley
were an island
held and bound
by the river flow
of stone
and when
in summer rain
white limestone
turns black
and the central green
is light-wracked
round the edges
that dark
reflective gleam
of rock
becomes
an edging brilliance
that centers
each field
to deep emerald.

No other place
I know
speaks
simultaneously
of meadows
and desert,
absorbing dryness
and winter wet,
the ground
porous and forgiving
of all elements,
white and black,
wet and dry,
rich and barren,
like a human
marriage,
one hand
of welcome
raised,
the other
tightened
involuntary
on a concealed
knife in the
necessary
protections
of otherness.

As if someone
had said, you will
learn
in this land
the same welcome
and the same exile
as you do in your
mortal vows
to another,
you will promise
yourself
and abase yourself
and find yourself
again
in the intimacy
of opposites,
you will pasture yourself
in the living green
and the bare rock,
you will find
comfort in strangeness
and prayer
in aloneness,
you will be proud
and fierce
and single minded

even
in your unknowing
and you will
carry on
through all the seasons
of your living
and dying
until
your aloneness
becomes equal
to the trials
you have set yourself.

Then this land
will become again
the land
you imagined
when you saw it
for the first time
and these vows
of marriage
can become
again and again
the place you
make your
residence
like
this same
rough
intimate
and cradled
ground

between
stone horizons,
embracing,
and also
always
like her,
beyond you,
strangely beautiful
to know
by its distance.

[V]
CHANCES

THE SWANS AT
GLEANN TREASNA

Above the lake
now
the bright
staggered arrival
of swans
against the mountain,
each one
breasting
the gusty damp air
at dusk.

They trouble
the water only
for a braced
moment
then fold
together into
three steadying
images
of floating
whiteness,
their feathers
roughening
in the wind
this way and that,
their necks
assuming
that familiar curve
of crested
contentment

seeing in their
own
reflections
the first instinctual
recognition
of arrival.

They feather
the water
in curves
across the lake,
the cold surface
encouraging them
to a definitive
reflective whiteness,
marking them
in a textured
silvered
hallmark grace
like ruffled
almost forgotten
heroes
come home
to claim
contentment.

And I watch
in the cold
at the edge
of the lake
spell-bound
and awkward,
observing
from a stumbling
humanity
how they skim
all troubling
elements
of air and water
and trouble myself
in compensation
with old stories
of their
coming
and going,
their absences
and their observed
faithful
reunions

and remember
how we look
each summer
for the first
glad sight
of new cygnets
trailing the broken
waters
behind them.
But the way,
firstly,
we fill
their mythologies
with exile,
with
absent white
disguises
and with
their trapped
need for a human
sisterly help.

The way
we need to describe
their long flights
over wracked seas,
nine years this way
and nine years that
and then after
so we won't
die
of the cold

unmoving loneliness
centered
in the stories
we've assigned them,
their home-comings,
their wanton
bewitched
love of strange horizons
no longer necessary,
their changeling
half-magic
provenance
of the air
become earthly
magic
arrived
and real,
their found reflections
not just
a new surface
but the depth
and plumb
of the element
that holds them.

The frontier
they inhabit
in the sky
or in the water
become
a found freedom
again.

To us
it's
the gift
of knowing
that white
feathered
reflective
graced
and utterly silent
conversation
between a fixed
self
and a no self.

THE FOX
(For Doris Kareva)

I remember the fox
and your train to the east,
two travellers, secret, and alone
in mutual recognition,
the eyes, the ears,
the wild red fur,
your look of surprise
at the sudden, tawny, flash
across the road,
knowing then, in the fox, the journey,
the way forward,
and our instincts already like him,
fugitive, glimpsed, already at bay,
you ready to stay or go
into what you loved,
your arrival in my life
so sudden and then
so quickly
your final disappearance.

WHEN THE WIND FLOWS

When the wind flows
and the leaves fall
and your own death
comes to greet you
with its slack mouth

you'll have to ask
forgiveness then
to gain an easy conscience
for the road ahead,
otherwise,
no one will want you
where he comes from.

No, it's not that they're choosy,
it's just that you wouldn't be happy
without his earnest advice
on the learned and
slightly desperate disciplines
of letting go,
no, you wouldn't
get anywhere near the place
without realising
what you'd been missing all along.

He knows you well enough,
he knows you want
the burden to be yours
and yours alone,
and he knows you'd prefer
a hundred hells than a heaven
where you can't cover with a smile
what until now you've hidden
and never spoken in the clear air.

That's why you'll be terrified
when he first arrives and hell
you realize resembles more
an average life,
half hidden,
never fully spoken,
something you can grow used to.

[VI]
RETURNS

THE THICKET

The tangle of it all, the briar curve perspective,
the entrance to places you could not go
without being tugged at the edges, caught
by tiny infractions of wool on the sweater,
brought to a twisted halt to unhook.

I would go anyway in old clothes,
free and happy through a necessary wounding,
my knees damp with the earth, the taste of blood
in my mouth like a richer earth.

In the thicket I could be free and observant,
surveying the tiny stages and the curtained dramas,
every further stage of vision leading me back
to smaller and smaller worlds, like a child's
telescoping theater guiding the eye to a tiny backdrop.
In one, I still see the wren, pivoting straight up
on a branch end, in another, the sloes burn on,
calm and content in their soft black light.
I was never afraid in the thicket, never cramped
or contained and even the constrained scurry
of something close but invisible in the brush brought
home to me all the rewards of a sheltered, secret life.
No one knew me in my child's aloneness
by any other names but the ones that called me back
to the quiet den I made in the hedge
and it seemed with this rich, impassable, interiority
all outer revelation was possible. From those shadows
I looked happily over great green spaces where
an open visibility would render me unseen.

All that summer I thought I could make it last,
never leave the branching world where, permanent
in my innocence, I could sit, a child abroad beyond
the house and call of waving neighbours,
a crouched pilgrim, an apprentice to stealth and
silence,
still and sovereign at the center of my shadowed world,
a kind of enclosed womb-like eternity that could
end only with the annunciation that another wider
and wiser eternity was about to begin.

All of that summer as I changed unknowingly
from young boy to young man, as I went in secret
from undifferentiated shadow to clear edged caster
of a shadow, I looked and looked and changed
unknowingly by looking, afraid as it all began
of the strange impatience growing behind my eyes,
the wound of desire opening slowly at the center
of my sight, not knowing at first that that looking
was a new kind of looking, that that dry mouth
of anticipation was prelude to a different form
of speech, that that minute searching of the
stained glass light searching between the branches
was the knowledge of some immanence
I could not imagine, come to find me
until I half felt, half met, the guiding signal
telling me to leave.

Something fought and sought and found me
in the hedge, gripped me with a new intelligence,
arrested me and set me to motion,
brought clarity to silence, set me to grow
and take this body out of hiding,
made me see the shadows stir with new
and revelatory intolerance, the hooked briars
raw with dispensation and beckoning.

An opening in my world come to find me,
bring me out. Some guiding hand lifted
and shone on me, found me in outline,
illumined the way I shaped in the light,
passed on − the red haw of a new season,
swung like a lantern through the sheltering dark.

MARINER

Surrounded by stones and trees
and circling the village on foot
we saw the tense wind begin to swirl
red leaves among the roots
and tasted at last in our mouths
the first dry culminating dust
of a summer's end.

I realized then
the sudden annunciation,
the quick beginning all at once
of something that had
until now only a slow
interior formation,
and I turned my face naturally
into the eye of that wind,
like the keel of some intuitive vessel
rearing toward the
source of the blow,
from that direction
I felt impending danger
and freedom and even across that
interior landscape
the whole sway
and fetch of a sea.

Above me, peacocks
screamed on a high wall
stretching their necks
to the bronze-shot clouds,
the chestnut trees
shook their leaves in a mass,
then above them,
a skyward rustle of doves
like upswung leaves,
a quick, tightening of the throat
and the full storm broke upon us
like a wave.

The whole world
was movement then
even before the first
premonitory clap
of thunder rolled across the Downland
and I, young again in the involuntary
necessities of a rough creation
ran off and left the path,
found shelter from the sudden searing light
in the door of a barn piled with bales
and the pungent yeast of decaying straw.

Separated from friends and glad to be alone,
forty six and looking for some secret
memory I'd hidden from myself,
the air freshening even as it frightened,
the heart alive and broken open
to its own sudden, unloved
and necessary demise.

The robust inclinations of a spirit
long covered by necessity began
to touch a future still waiting
to be met. In the reek
of hay and the upward whirl of dust,
I felt youth again, not as memory
now but a forceful anticipation,
something yet to come.
As if the hand of someone
once alive in the memory
had reached through confusion
and touched me again.
The horizon all implication
and extended invitation
to sudden arrival.
All the elemental forces
of the world a pure revelation.
This day my life,
this body a ground
on which to stand,
this weather a sea,
and my sense of self
a strange shoreline
on which it broke and fell.

My hand lifted to parse the light.
I remembered kneeling as a child
over the new worlds I'd seen charted
on a blank and open page,
me there on the kitchen floor,
a small devoted figure
reading Coleridge over and over,
my bent head
compelled to the fearful journey
like an intuited prayer for my whole life,
some child in me
abroad in the storm
inclined once more
to the old wonder
and my heart moved to write it all again.

SLIGO GLEN:
WALKING INTO SILENCE

Imagine a path before you
and imagine as you walk it
the path worn deeper and deeper
into the ground so that
as it beckons you further
into the narrow valley and
under the roof of spreading trees,
the sides of the path
rear up to hold you
and enclose you and the walls
of this path are white stone covered
with ivy and lichen and green moss
and that by walking this path
into the enclosed earth
you had entered a pure,
innocent and hidden silence
for which you realize
amid the noise and tumult
of your own creation,
you had waited years.

Then you would be
in The Glen, near Sligo Town,
at the edge of the sea
about to cross a threshold
into some life
you had once called your own
and as you walked
into the dark mouth
of the valley you could marvel
at the utter,

exuberant exclusion
of human sound
and at the shelter extended
by its sombre tree shadowed silence
and in the center of those shadows
penumbral to your own body
you could catch sight above
of clear stars even at midday
and feel reflected
inside you, even through
a troubled surface
an equivalent and burning symmetry
waiting to be read.
And then, as if
that text was being spoken
as you walked
and as if you were listening
yourself from the center
of some silent fire,
and as if from nowhere
and as if from some
other correspondence
to your journey into the earth
you could hear in that
forgotten script
some old necessity
for which you had been
waiting,
long years
and it would be
again

as if the sun
had risen for you
from ashes and from greyness
and blessed you
as you went
shaking off the clinging
flakes of darkness
and in you grew
a clear lighted
view over an open landscape,
and it could be dawn again
and the fields new ploughed
and the larks alive in the minted air,
and you could find in that opening
silence that after all
you had not forgotten
that your memory was true
and that your faith
had been something alive and
therefore deserving of failure,
it was
like everything else in the world
bound to stall and stutter
and go out
to leave you orphaned
and alone in the dark
so that you would
look afresh for the original
light of your own parentage.
To find it new again,
like this.

SLIGO GLEN:
WALKING OUT OF SILENCE

And then, after,
when you'd turned back
by the way you came,
back toward
the mouth of the Glen
you'd entered
noisily just an hour before,
calling to the others
and you reached again,
but this time alone
the invisible line
where
you could mark exactly
when you began to hear
the sounds of the road
and the machines and the blank
cries of everyday commerce,
so that for a moment you could
retrace that one single step
back into the Glen
and immerse yourself
instantly
in the quiet
source of revelation
you had felt
only a moment before,

as if under water,
as if slipping back
into the river
of silence running between
the tree lined walls
and then you could practice
leaving and
returning in your own body,
through your own breath,
inward and outward,
descending and
entering and reentering the silence
and shelter of your own
narrow valley of aloneness,
from interiority
to conversation
and back.

So that you suddenly realized
you were given
the complete and utter gift
of your own transparency,

the revelation of your
own exact boundary with
the world.

The frontier
between silence and speech
exactly
the line you must cross
to give yourself
while saving yourself,

the gleam in your heart
and your eye,
another sun rising,
the old memories alive
after a long night of absence
and the world again
suddenly worth
risking,
worth seeing,
worth innocence,
worth everything.

The glittering tines of the young
white-tailed buck
silhouetted by a sunlit marsh.

The sheer entrancing
beauty of the thing
standing coal-black in a halo of dew.

Impossible to believe this wildness
just a mile
from the airport hotel.

That I woke this morning
looking over that barren nothing
of parked cars and endless concrete,

that I expected to run nourished
by my breath but not my eyes
round some grey circle and back.

But seeing my reflection
in the glass door
of the hotel, I turned back

I don't know why,
and asked the two young women
standing behind the desk

if they knew a green place
close by for me to run
and of course they knew

no such place,
but they seemed to part
even as they said this

to let another
more purposeful woman stride
from the back

and direct me, with grace
and a noble, uncalled for
intelligence,

Left by the south parking lot
take the road and turn into the trees.
You'll find the reserve.

You know, I must remember,
until my last breath goes out
to ask. To try, every time, one last time

to confirm the native
human intuition that heaven
is never far away at all,

that it's just a door or a step
or a whole short life to get there.
I must remember

to stop people on the street
as if the most closed,
grey, concrete, commuting life

could be just a skim
on the pool
of communal revelation

and as if, in my continued hurry
I just haven't
given anyone or anything

anywhere, any time
to let me know
what's really about to happen,

to catch my reflection
looking quizzically back at me
before I go through the wrong door,

the door where I forgot to ask
before I entered.
I must remember

to knock on other doors,
to call out people's names,
to enquire as if my life

depended on knowing
that something
always lies close

and to remember that it takes
only one requited request
for the extraordinary

to make a hundred ordinary
encounters
up to that moment

more than extraordinary,
rare, numinous,
a harvest

worth having,
no matter how difficult
to sow and reap.

And that the angel always
has to elbow her way
toward us

through a lot of unknowing
toward our plain
complacent ignorance,

so that when
I'm on
my hospital bed

surrounded by
those I know,
or if in the end

I go alone
and forsaken,
or taken by surprise,

in the high windows
of some
great national tragedy,

I'll remember
just before I go
to reach out and ask

for a good place to go.
I'll reach out my hand
to another door

and find myself surprised
by the way it was
there all along,

just around the corner
from the immobile place
I stood just a moment before.

So that when I jump
something will be there
I couldn't imagine.

You think I am speaking
of paradise, but no,
I am thinking of the life

we leave behind
made splendid
by the courage of our going.

The way every going
in the world,
no matter how difficult,

is an inheritance
for those
still left to witness.

This stag for instance,
waiting in a halo
of its own nobility,

about to run
into the September
mist,

my fears for the blank greyness
of the world dissolved
by its innocence

risking itself for me.
Like the angel of a bright day
I had not foreseen

beckoning from that clear
and cloudless September sky
calling me to a time

and a place
and a meeting
I am not prepared to know.

THE BELL RINGER

Consider the bell
ringer as an image
of the human soul,
he stands foursquare
on the stone flagged
ground, and surrounded
by a circle of communal
concentration
searches in his fixed
aloneness
for a world
beyond straight,
human,
eye to eye
discourse,
in this case
above him,
the collision of metal
worlds chiming
to each bend and lift
of the knees,
letting his weight
bear down
on the rope,
creating out of the heave
and upward pull,
a hollowed out
brass utterence,
a resonant
on-going argument
for his continued presence,
independent

of daily mood
or the necessities
for a verbal
proclamation.

Consider the reason
for his continued
attendance
to the art.
Caught in a committed
circle of constant practice
yet freed in the vertical
from a horizontal
ever present
and exhausting
human participation,
the ultimate arbitration
an over arching,
straight-out
relationship
with sound.

Somewhere above
in the vertical
he touches
another firmament,
his face
lined, preoccupied
or even set
against the world,
can still announce joy
in the sweet resonance

of birth,
or drama
in the long,
extended,
over and over
carillions of
marriage.

No matter
the clarity
or cloudiness
of the day,
he can follow
that out-going tide
of sound right
to the very edge
of the circled
horizon
until it ebbs back
around him
into the center
of things,
pooling
to a more
rhythmic toll,
a deeper,
more concentrated
commemoration,
the knelling way
the world sounds
inside

when
we've heard
the ease and release
of a last breath.

Let him stand there
then
for the human soul,
let his weight
come true on the rope,
the way we want to lean
into the center of things,
the way we want to
fall with the gravity
of the situation
and then afterwards
laugh and
defy it
with an upward
ultimately untraceable
flight,
a great ungovernable
ringing
announcement
to the world
that
something, somewhere,
has changed.

Consider
the bellringer
as one of us,
attempting some

unachieved,
magnificent
difference in the world,
far above
and far beyond
the stone-closed
space
we seem
to occupy.

Below
we're all
effort, listening
and
wilful concentration,
above,
like a moving sea,
another power
shoulders
just
for a moment
the whole burden,
lifts us
against our will,
lets us find
in the skyward pull
a needed antidote
to surface noise,
a gravity against gravity,
another way to hear
amid
the clamor of the heavens.